Once More with Feeling:
Poems by Arnold David Richards

ONCE MORE WITH FEELING

Poems by Arnold David Richards

International Psychoanalytic Books

New York • http://www.IPBooks.net

Once More with Feeling: Poems by Arnold David Richards
Published by IPBooks, Queens, NY
Online at IPBooks.net

Cover layout by Kathy Kovacic, Blackthorn Studio
Interior design and layout by Noel S. Morado

Cover Painting: Sophie Taeuber-Arp, *Aubette 182*, 1927.

ISBN 978-1-969031-17-5

Contents

Once More with Feeling

Once more with feeling
But then with meaning
Feelings first
And words come next
That's how we connect
That's how we relate
That's how we express
Our concern for each other
That is what life is about
Relating
Caring
Loving
Doing
Being
Always

Consciousness and Selfhood

Consciousness

5

To be conscious
Is to be alive
To act
To choose
To do
To live
In the world
Pleasure
And satisfaction
Creating
Agency
Opportunity
To cherish
Not to miss
Waking
Is better than
Sleeping
But nothing
Lasts forever
I am not afraid
Of death
Woody Allen said
As long as I am not
There when it happens

Familiarity

We like the familiar
Repetition
The same
Again and again
Comforting
But there has
to be a place for innovation
Without innovation
There is stagnation
Progress stops
Boredom takes over
Familiarity
Should breed contempt
We need to keep on our toes
The world presents
Many challenges
Physical
Political
Psychological
Hopefully
Young people
The next generation
Will be up to the task
Our children will save us

Humanity

Rest on four pillars
Fairness
Morality
Diversity
Justice

How we get along with each other
Mutual concern
Empathy
All necessary

Aggression

Aggression on the football field
Is better than aggression on
The battlefield
Nobody dies
In the Olympics
The Greeks had it right
Aggression sublimated
Trophies not
Caskets
Win or lose
Play another game

Conscience

We need our conscience
To keep us on the straight and narrow
Morality
Is the highest value
Compassion is a virtue
Kindness is a priority
Being nice to each other
Makes life worth living
Helps us to appreciate each other
And reach for the stars

Permanence or Change

A paradox
Permanence or change
Permanence necessary
For continuity
Change necessary
For development
Can we have both?
We can if we stick to
Our foundational principles
Our moral center
Difficult
Because of selfishness
Greed
Immorality
Religion should help
But it doesn't
Wise leaders
Should make a difference
Where are they?
They are in short supply
We can only depend on each other
On those we trust
On those we care about
Those who care about us
Everything else
Is commentary
No more to say

Personal Coordinates

My personal coordinates
Not my GPS
My place in my moral world
The boundaries of my humanity
Relationships with friends
And family
Do I do unto others?
As I would have others do to me
What about philanthropy?
Do I give as much as I can?
Do I help others as much as I can?
Is there someone watching?
Observing
Taking notes
Making judgments
But what counts most?
Is my own judgment
What is right for me?
Who I am
And who I want to be

Where I Have Been

And where am I going?
I have been around the world
Visited many places
Seen a lot
Done a lot
More to do
More poems to write
Writing poetry is
A gift I am grateful for
Book six
Once more with feeling
Feeling is first
All the people
I care about
Family and friends
A full life
More to come

What Keeps a Man Alive

13

He gives to others
If you have enough
For yourself
You can share
With others
Altruism
Selflessness
Good works
Are appreciated
Wealth may be limited
Wisdom is not
Knowledge
Is accumulated
From experience
The test of time

Health and Happiness

14

Go hand and hand
Can you have one
Without the other?
Hard to be happy
When you are sick
More unhappiness
More illness
A sound mind
In a sound body
A good life

Serenity

We all long for serenity
Hard to achieve
In this turbulent world
Conflicts abound
At home and abroad
Hard to find
Those you can trust
Many are driven
By their own self interest
But what is good for one
Is often good for all
The long view
Is at the best approach
Start with family
And friends
And then broaden
Your horizons
Good luck

Being Human

Is a problem we all share
The heights
Of our excellence
And the depths
Of our depravity
Morality
Is fragile
Temptations abound
Pleasures are ephemeral
Satisfactions limited
Love does not cure all
Staying healthy
Is difficult
Some of us
Are more lucky
Than others
Some live longer
Some die younger
Is it chance
Or design?
The luck of the draw

Meaning

What is the meaning of life?
Does life have meaning?
An important question
Meaning for who?
For me or
Meaning for you
It depends on who you care for
On what you care about
That is what makes life meaningful
Who do you live for?
Or what would you die for?
Not easy questions to answer
For me It is a matter of day to day
What I do some days
Is more meaningful
Than what I do on other days
I live in the moment
I remember the past
But I think about the future
There is hope
Say the brown bells
Of Merthyr

Stop the World

I want to get off
but I can't of course
I live under constraints
Time place
History
Ethnicity
I do the best
I can
Real
Limitations
How many
Degrees
Of freedom
Do I have?
Body and mind
Hard to accept
I want it all

The Oral Triad

19

To sleep
To dream
To eat
To be eaten
The oral triad
Plus one
Elemental
Existential
The essence
Of my unconscious
Moves me
Without my awareness
Consciousness
Is an epiphenomena
On the surface
Removed
From whom I really am

Arts and Sciences

Things Come and Go

Appear and disappear
Here today
Gone tomorrow
That is how
My world is
I long for permanence
But can't find it
I go back
and forth
But there are some things
That last
Art of course
Shakespeare has been around
A long time
I enjoy watching a
Shakespeare play
That I have seen many times
Music
Rossini
Barber of Seville
Yesterday
And a year ago
Painting
Mona Lisa
Her smile
Doesn't go away
Picasso painting

Girl before the mirror
Painted in 1932
She looks out at me
She will be there
For an eternity
She will
I won't

My Muse

___

25

I have an inner voice
I don't know it's source
I don't know it's origin
It compels me
It impels me
Inspires me
I see the world
In my own light
My private view
Like no other
Special unique
And particular
My priorities
Developed over many years
A wealth of experience
And more to come

Photography

Photography
Makes art
Out of the ordinary
The photographer's
Eye is crucial
The photographer's
Sensibility
Is unique
An eye for design
Enters into every
Composition
Content should be
Meaningful
A window on
The human condition
A window on my
Humanity
I will collect
My photographs
And publish them
For all to see

Science

Plank said science advances
One funeral at a time
What we don't know
Is as important
Or even more important
Than what we do know
Proof does not come easy
Certainty is elusive
Artificial intelligence
May be just that
Artificial not substantive
It may be a siren song
And give us a false sense of certainty
In my opinion
There is no substitute
For human intelligence
For the rigors of human reason
Hypothesis testing
And confirmation
Artificial intelligence
May be a slippery slope
A road taken
With much for thought
And skepticism
I can be accused of being
A nay sayer
But rather safe than sorry

Quantum Uncertainty

Quantum uncertainty
Is a game changer
For our orderly universe
The universe bubbles
Light is propagated
In all directions
Nothing is predictable
No cause and effect
How do we find a place
To stand?
We are able go about our business
Despite the uncertainty
Because we are a small part
Of a much bigger picture
What is certain?
Health and sickness
Rich and poor
Democracy and autocracy
Free and enslaved

Universe

The sky
Is my theater
Every night there
Is a performance
Aurora Borealis
Blood moon
Comets
Shooting stars
The endless expanse
Of the sky
What we see
Started out
Light years before
And arrives
After a very long
Journey
The planets
Each with an evocative
Mythical name
Mercury speed
Venus love
Mars war
Jupiter
Saturn and its
Rings
Neptune the sea
Uranus

And Pluto
Too far too see
The expanse of the sky
Surely
Our humility
Continuity
What we see
Many, many. before us
Have seen

Wikipedia

Wikipedia
Is the wonder
Of the modern world
Everything we know
Is in it
And google
Enables us
To find
Everything we
Need to know
Knowledge
Is our universe
Our world
Defines us
Mastery
Empowerment
We are in charge
Pick up your pens
Interact
Communicate
We need to rock
The boat
To create
A better world

Nature

Seed

How does the seed know
What it's supposed to become
Programmed
Etched in stone
A leaf
A tree
A strawberry
Lilles of the valley
Nature gives
The leaf no choice
What has to be
Will be

Let it Snow, Let it Snow, Let it Snow

Here today
Gone tomorrow
A white blanket
Covers New York
For me now
Memory
Not reality
Do I miss it?
Maybe

Palm Beach

37

Is paradise
The weather
Is nice
Every day
Better
And better
Enjoy

Love

Love

41

Love can be ephemeral
Deep or superficial
A passing fancy
Or a lifelong commitment
It is the ultimate treasure
A deep pleasure
Can last every day
Challenged always
Sustaining
Takes effort
True to one self
True to the other
Every day
Can be St Valentine's Day
A holiday
For some fortunate few

Anniversary

Another year
Another anniversary
Another milestone
Many have gone
More to come
Love
And fulfillment
Happiness
Over the brim
Substantial
Consequential
Special
Ours
Alone
To savor
For a lifetime
Lucky us

Valentine's Day

43

Valentines Day is Love
Love is Valentines Day
Caring
Sharing
Concerned
Alway
Quote
The raven
Ever more

Life

Life

Life
Is now
Not yesterday
Or tomorrow
The past is gone
The future has not
Arrived
The challenge is
What we get
Done today
24 hours
Is not forever
Enough time
I make a difference
In our life
And the lives
Of others

Life 2

We begin life
With the conviction
That we will live forever
But that belief
Doesn't last forever
Denial persists
But the end becomes
Less frightening
Woody Allen said
I am not afraid
If I am not there
When it happens
Illness changes
Our perception
We mellow
And can
Better accept
The inevitable
Some can
More than others
Time is precious
And should
Be cherished

My Life

49

I look back at my life
And I found it hard to understand
How much I have done
How many books I have published
How many papers I have written
and how many poems I authored
How I have helped as many patients
As I have
All done without deliberation
It feels like it just happened
Without forethought
That is how the best
Things in life happen
In the spaces
When you go with the flow
And let the spirit move you
To where you will go

Luck

50

Life is lottery
And luck is the lady
Of the night
Win lose or draw
Everyone has their turn
I don't mind that
Choice or chance
All a matter of the odds
But the house has the edge
And prevails
Most of the time

Generosity

Generosity is a virtue
A profound value
It reflects our care for other people
It comes from the best part of us
And should be cherished
And valued more than many other traits
We should give to others
Not just to have others return to us
Sharing and caring
Go together
If that was a common priority
And moved our life
Happiness for all
It starts in the family
It starts with our children
It continues with our friends
It is central to the human compact

Memory

52

My mind is filled with
Memory
From the sublime
To the ordinary
Yesterday
And decades ago
The banal
And the profound
From within
And from my surround
The most cherished
About those I love
Family and friends
The big picture
And the small details

My Parents

Died many years ago

They would have been more than 100 years old today.

I have very fond memories of them and my brother and sister as well. We were very engaged with each other through thick and thin, up and down. Life was always a struggle, making a living was very hard, but there was lots and lots of love which made all the difference. I don't think there was much rivalry between myself and my sister. I was the favorite, and my sister seemed to accept that very willingly. I was special for both my mother and my father and for everyone else in the family. There was economic, poverty, but emotional plenty. I was lucky growing up in that kind of privileged background. I was idolized by my teachers and by my classmates I was elected president every year from the first grade to the sixth grade, and I was often given their responsibility to run the class instead of the teacher. My privileged position was a matter of course for me. It was how I saw in the world. Reading was my passion. I would go through the encyclopedia volume by volume cover to cover. I wanted to learn everything to know everything and always be first in my class.

Money and Me

Money and me
Who I am
The main value
Money has for me
Is being able to give it away
To family
And philanthropy
Money has limited
Personal value
Some money
Or more money
Doesn't provide
As much personal satisfaction
As writing a single poem
As this one

Where I have Been

55

And where am I going
I have been around the world
Visited many places
Seen a lot
Done a lot
More to do
More poems to write
Writing poetry is
A gift I am grateful for
Book six
Once more with feeling
Feeling is first
All the people
I care about
Family and friends
A full life
More to come

What Goes Around

56

Comes around
Whatever we do
Has consequences
Banal and
Profound
We live in a community
All with our own
Interests
All with our own
Priorities
Often hard to accept
The needs of others
Other than the needs of our own
Forging a social contract
Is a very difficult
Communal task

Our House

57

Each one of us
Have two houses
The house in our neighborhood
And the house which is the universe
We live in both of them
At the same time
Each provides a different vantage point
One smaller
One larger
Different perspectives
We see with different eyes
Binary vision
Keeps us
On track

The Golden Rule

The golden rule
Is banal on the surface
But profound underneath
it is central to our social contract
The rules we live by
What makes us human
Concern for others
and for our selves
The challenge is to
Teach it to our children
And for our children to teach it to their children
A lifetime challenge

Seasons

59

The year has seasons
Spring
Childhood
Summer
Adolescence
Fall
Maturity
Winter
Old age
And life has stages
Learning
Loving
Earning
Creating
Each in its season
Alone
And together
We look
Forward
To the future
As we remember
The past
We widen our world
Expand our orbit
Mark our accomplishments
Consolidate our achievements
Leave our legacy

For our posterity
We will not be
Forgotten after we
Are gone

Life's Landmarks

61

Circumcision was
the first
Entering the
Covenant
No idea
What it meant
School next
Bar mitzvah
Mariage
Three baby
Carriages
Parents pass
Grand children
Great grand children
And many generations
Follow
Continuity

Wisdom

62

Wisdom takes a lifetime
To acquire
A lifetime of experience
And the lifetime of relationships
Science is important
But common sense
Is also essential
The deep and profound
Not superficial
What we don't know
Is also important
Truth is not easy
To come by
Many fall starts
Searching for consensus

Aspiration

What moves us
What drives me
What I feel
Will make my
Life better
In fantasy
And reality
Needs to be
Made conscious
I need to acquire
What I aspire for
Recognition
Worldly goods
Relationships
More than
Anything else
To love
And be loved
For a life time
Family
And friends
Our world

Memory 1

64

I think of my mother
I think of my father
Often
They took care of me
I took care of them
I miss them very much
But I remember many
Experiences
As if they were just
Yesterday
They came from an old culture
Immigrants
The old world
I was born here
A new culture
The new world
More comfortable for me
Than for them
I think they learned
More from me
Than I learned
From them
I became the doctor
My father wanted
To be

My mother's pride
And joy
We made a life
Together

Memory 2

My mind is very sharp
Which is a blessing
If you use it
You won't lose
I like to remember
Names from the past
Remembering is a challenge
I like to pass
It sometimes
Takes a while
But I do
More often
Than not

Politics

Politics

Politics
Is a pendulum
Swings from right to left
and left to right
From left to right
In Europe
Hungary, Germany, France
And from right to left
Hopefully in my country
In the United States
Those in charge
Are losing support
Murder in Minnesota,
Hoping for a popular uprising
Anti ICE demonstrations
The people will speak
Democracy
Will prevail

Passions

Remorse
Regret
Retribution
And revenge
How we relate
To each other
Sometimes
But tempered
With kindness
And mercy
True to ourselves
Makes us proud
But not always
Popular
Standing up
For what we
Believe in
And what we
Stand for

A New Birth of Freedom

In the Gettysburg address, Lincoln refers to the God-given right for a new birth of freedom. I think freedom was as important to Lincoln has mercy, and an absence of malice. The quest for freedom was what the war of independence was about and remains central to our national DNA. Freedom to innovate, freedom to regulate, freedom to govern ourselves is what drives us now, but is under attack by those in charge. Freedom requires a rule of law. Freedom is a cause to die for. Freedom must be our highest priority and not to be compromised in any way

For Lincoln's Birthday

In his second inaugural address
Lincoln said "With malice toward none
And charity for all"
I don't know if I can agree with that
I have malice toward the murderers
Of my 6 million coreligionists
And no mercy for the perpetrators
Many who met no punishment
After the war
I can think of few people
In my everyday life that I have
Malice for but that may because of
Who I choose to associate with
Mercy is another matter
My cup runeth over
And I have a lot
Of good feelings
To share with
Many other people
I have compassion
For the ill and infirm
helping others
For me is a way of fife
Learned from my parents

Our Country

Immigration
Or deportation
Emma Lazarus
Or Donald Trump
A country that betrays its values
Loses its legitimacy
Loses its reason for being
We may be
At a point of no return
The beginning of economic downturn
As well as moral decline
Many want to leave
But don't know where to go
Canada
Scandinavia perhaps
Israel, but its right wing government
Is also problematic
Or we could stay at home
Remain and try to make a difference
Not easy, but it may be our only choice
Midterm elections
2028
There may be hope for the future
Say the brown bells
Of Myrther

Survival

74

How do we survive
In this cruel world
We have a president addicted to power
Who acquired for himself
A pseudo Nobel prize
A Supreme Court that
Enables all his unconstitutional
Activity
A Congress that won't stand up
For the rule of law
For ordinary people
For what is right
And there is the silent
Majority that won't speak up
That won't act
We can wait for the next election
But a lot of bad stuff
Can happen before that
I am a Cassandra
I make true prophecies
That no one believes
If Trump is allowed to continue
On the course that he has set out on
Our world order
Will be seriously disrupted

End of NATO
End of our alliances
The triumph of Russia and China
Our country beware
Sleepers awake
Protest
Agitate
March to the barricades

Leaders

We need leaders
Who have a moral center
With out such leaders we are lost
We live in very dangerous times
The pendulum is swinging
Dangerously to the right
Autocratic leaders are on the ascendancy
The hope for the future
Is the next election
Which may save us
And then begin the process
To save the world

Political Discourse

The challenge we face
Is how to communicate
In advance, our body politic
The problem is that the blame game
Seems to be central to our discourse
Dialogue is polarized
Right and wrong
Good and bad
It is hard for us to have
Conversations
About fundamental issues
And fundamental principles
Freedom fairness
Equality diversity
The rule of law
Need to be our watch words
Our aim should be
To develop a consensus
About these matters
I think the problem is
We have an establishment
That needs to remain in charge
No one in power gives up power willingly
The ballot box decides

The current administration
Makes voting more difficult
Requires more identification
A disaster might follow
Rubio is talking to Urban
Is Urban the kind of autocratic dictator
That Trump wants to emulate?

Stephen Miller

Stephen Miller is worse
Than Charlie Kirk
Closer to power
They're going around taking names
Taking your father's name
Taking your mother's name
Taking your sister's name
Fascism is the name
ICE murder
That is our country now
Who is to blame?

26

In 26 the sky was red
Thunder rumbling overhead
And on that frosty morn
The orange man who would be king
Couldn't sleep in his bed
And our democracy was gone

God Help Us

Everyone
Crisis in our country
Constitution in tatters
Trump goes after Powell
Who is next
No one is safe
Who will take a stand
Who will lead us
Midterm elections
Our only hope
I am not holding
My breath
ICE in the streets
Murder every where
Who is next?
Is there hope
For our future?
Not a good
Century
For my country

My Childhood

82

Who knows
What evil lurks
In the heart of man?
The shadow knows
The 20th century
Hitler Stalin
Nazi Germany
And the Soviet Union
The 21st-Century,
Russia
And the US
Ukraine
Nicaragua
Evil more
Acknowledged
Always there

These Are the Times that Try Men's Souls

Where is our 21st-century Thomas Paine?
We need him desperately
Him or her
Someone
Who will save us?
Patriot
Not fair-weather friends

Impeachment

Trump is putting
Our country
Our constitution
And our alliances
In great danger
He is held hostage
Because of compromising
Information held by
Russia
He is also destroying
Our economy at home
While the Supreme Court
And Congress refuse
To act
Impeachment is the only
Remedy
The next Presidential election
Is too long to wait

May Day May Day May Day

85

Great danger
For our country
The orange man
Wants Greenland
He gets the war prize
NATO's demise

A President Run Amok

The orange man
Wants the Greenland
Malignant narcissism
Thirst for power
No concern for the world order
No concern for our neighbors and allies
No concern for our constitution
No concern for our country
No concern for democracy
No concern for the rule of law
Where is Congress?
Where is the Supreme Court?
Where is the majority?
Why doesn't it speak up?
Time is running out
As our President runs amok

The World

87

Is in terrible shape
We bombed Kharg island
Oil is going
Through the roof
The orange man
Is mad
A disaster
The center
Won't hold
The extremists
Take over
Billionaires
In charge
Will it get
Worse?

Trump

The orange man
Wants the Greenland
A boy wants
A toy to play with
Only cares about himself
About no other
He has brought us
To the brink
The end of NATO
The end of the Atlantic charter
The end of our mutual alliances
The Russians and the Chinese
Are laughing
As our ship sinks
Who is in charge at home?
Trump

Republican Congress
The right wing Supreme Court
Torpor
Indolence
Our country should be renamed
The Titanic
It was sad when the good ship went down
Sad

Titanic

Our country is the Titanic
And Trump is the iceberg
6/7 above water
All there for all to see
Little hidden
It was sad when that great ship went down
Women in children saved
The rest of us, drowned

World Order

Can one person undo the world order
In place since the end of WW II?
Occupying Greenland
Canada the 51 state
War ships steaming to the Middle East
Attacking Iran
Venezuela Colombia Cuba
The world is as frightening
As it ever has been
It is hard to concentrate
on ordinary every day concerns

Venezuela

We sold our soul
For oil
We opted for autocracy
Instead of democracy

Doomsday

Closer than ever
Climate change
Nuclear Armageddon
AI
Will we survive?
Hope

Corruption

There is corruption
In high places
In our country
There will be disruption
In our body politic
There will be a change
In those in charge
My prediction
The courts will judge
And elections will follow
The people will decide

Incomprehensible

The holocaust
Is incomprehensible
More than the numbers
The small details
What was done
Each day
The efficiency
Of the killing machine
Not an ounce of mercy
Not a modicum of concern
How can we understand
The motivations of the perpetrators?
How did they sleep at night?
How did they spend time with their family?
When they did what they did during the day
A group of Germans got together
And agreed on the final solution
Decided in one day
6 million murdered
Defies understanding
The depravity of individuals
Has it been equaled
Before or since?

Pride

95

Pride does not go
Before a fall
Pride is what we need
To stand tall
Personal pride
Ethnic pride
National pride
The last is in short supply
Instead of pride
We have denigration
Embarrassment
It is impossible
To feel proud
Of our president
It is impossible to feel proud
Of all those who support him
Of all those who voted for him
Of all those in Congress,
who will not stand up to him
But I am very proud
of everyone who does
That is my hope
That the country will turn around
In my lifetime